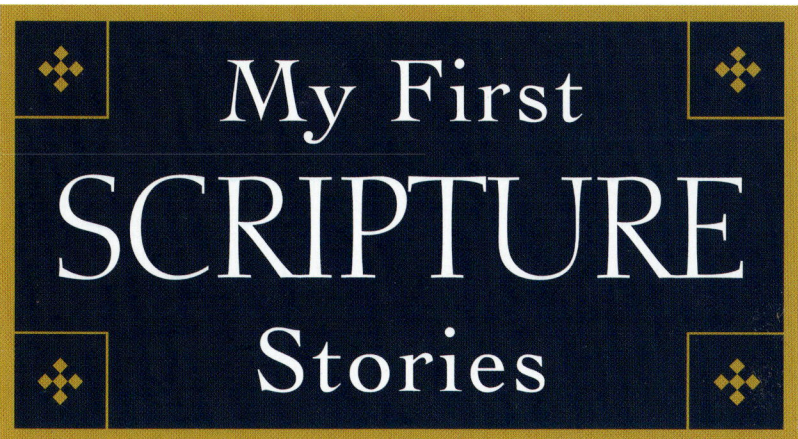

_____

This book belongs to

_____

Presented by

_____

Date

OTHER BOOKS BY DEANNA DRAPER BUCK

My First Book of the Latter-day Prophets

My First Book of Temples

My First Story of the First Christmas

My First Story of the First Easter

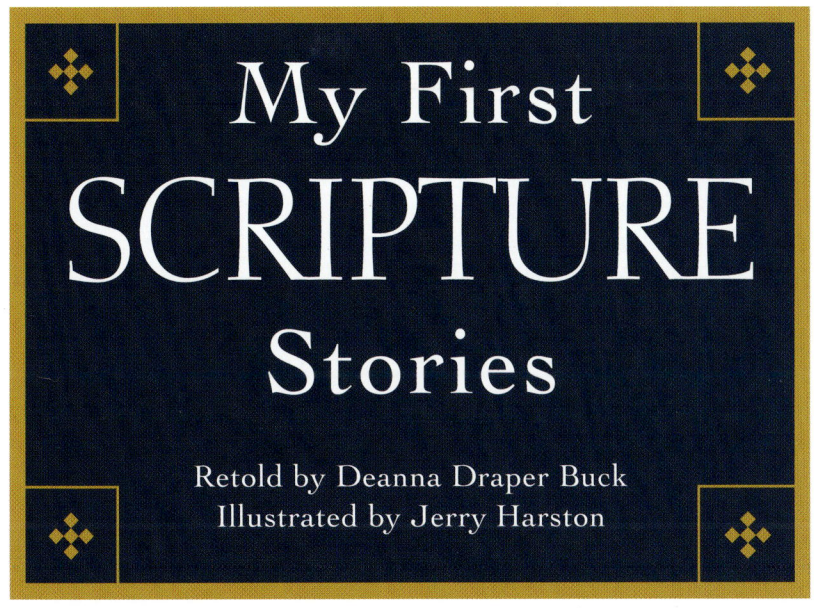

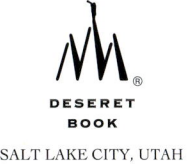
DESERET BOOK

SALT LAKE CITY, UTAH

Books in this compilation volume were previously published as follows:
My First Old Testament Stories (board book, 2001; paperback, 2010)
My First New Testament Stories (board book, 2002; paperback, 2009)
My First Book of Mormon Stories (board book, 1998)
More of My First Book of Mormon Stories (board book, 2005)
My First Church History Stories (board book, 1999; paperback, 2008)

Text © 2014 Deanna Draper Buck
Illustrations © Jerry Harston

All rights reserved. No part of this book may be reproduced in any form or by any means without permission in writing from the publisher, Deseret Book Company, at permissions@deseretbook.com or P. O. Box 30178, Salt Lake City, Utah 84130. This work is not an official publication of The Church of Jesus Christ of Latter-day Saints. The views expressed herein are the responsibility of the author and do not necessarily represent the position of the Church or of Deseret Book Company.

DESERET BOOK is a registered trademark of Deseret Book Company.

Visit us at DeseretBook.com

Library of Congress Cataloging-in-Publication Data

Buck, Deanna Draper, author.
  My first scripture stories / Deanna Draper Buck ; illustrated by Jerry Harston and Leslie Harston.
     pages cm
  ISBN 978-1-60907-948-2 (paperbound)
  1. Bible stories, English. 2. Book of Mormon stories, English. 3. The Church of Jesus Christ of Latter-day Saints—History—Juvenile literature. I. Harston, Jerry, illustrator. II. Harston, Leslie, illustrator. III. Title.
  BX8621.B83 2014
  289.3'32—dc23   2014031433

Printed in China
RR Donnelley, Shenzhen, China

10   9   8   7   6   5   4   3

To Weston, Arthor, Lilly, and Cormac ("Mort").
And to Jerry Harston—a huge thank-you for
your beautiful illustrations; each one is worth a
thousand words. You are loved and missed.

—DDB

Our Premortal Life

Long, long ago, before any of us were even born, we were all spirits. We lived together as brothers and sisters with our Heavenly Father. The time came when Heavenly Father told us that we were ready to go down to earth and receive bodies.

On earth we would learn how to choose the right and to love and help each other.

Jesus was chosen by Heavenly Father to be the creator of a beautiful world and to become our Savior. We were so happy that we all shouted for joy!

The Creation

Jesus made the world and everything in it. He made the mountains, the rivers and oceans, the clouds, the sun and moon and stars in the sky. He made all of the trees and plants and all of the animals.

When He was finished, the world was beautiful, and Heavenly Father said it was good.

Then Heavenly Father and Jesus created Adam and Eve, the first man and woman on the earth.

Adam and Eve

Adam and Eve lived in a beautiful place called the Garden of Eden. The Lord told them they could eat any of the fruit in the garden, except for the fruit of the Tree of Knowledge of Good and Evil. Satan was angry because he couldn't have a body, and he wanted to ruin God's plan. He tempted Adam and Eve to disobey Heavenly Father and eat the forbidden fruit. When they did so, Adam and Eve couldn't live in the Garden of Eden anymore.

Heavenly Father's Plan

After Adam and Eve left the Garden of Eden, an angel taught them about the Savior. The angel told them that if they would follow Jesus and live His teachings, then after Adam and Eve and their children died, they could all live with Heavenly Father again. Adam and Eve were happy to learn about the plan. They told their children about Jesus and taught them to love and help each other.

Noah

Noah was a prophet. He warned the people to obey God's commandments, but they would not listen to him. The Lord said He was going to destroy the wicked people and told Noah to build a large boat called an ark. Noah was told to take his family and two of each kind of animal into the ark.

Then it began to rain. Soon the earth was covered with water, but everyone on the ark was safe. After the flood was over, Heavenly Father made a rainbow in the sky as a sign He would never again cover the whole world with a flood.

The Tower of Babel

Many years after the flood, the world was filled with people once again. Some of the people were wicked and foolish. In their pride, they began to build a great city and a tower. They were not interested in the Lord or in keeping His commandments. The Lord was not happy with the people, and He confused their language so they couldn't talk to each other. He scattered them all over the world. A man named Jared and his family and friends loved the Lord, and their tongues were not confused. They were led by the Lord to the Americas, the promised land. You can read about them in the Book of Mormon.

Abraham and Isaac

Abraham loved his young son Isaac very much. One day the Lord told Abraham to sacrifice Isaac. Abraham did not want to do so, but he was obedient and took Isaac up a high mountain. Just as Abraham was ready to sacrifice Isaac, an angel stopped him. There was a sheep caught in some nearby bushes. Abraham sacrificed the sheep instead of Isaac. The angel told Abraham that the Lord was pleased with Abraham because he was willing to keep the commandments of God.

God's Covenant with Abraham

Because Abraham promised to love God and be obedient, the Lord made Abraham a special promise, called a covenant. Abraham was promised that Jesus would be born into Abraham's family;

that Abraham would have more people in his family than there are stars in the sky or grains of sand on the seashore; and that Abraham and his family would hold the priesthood and bless the whole world.

Joseph

Joseph was a good boy who loved Heavenly Father and tried to do what was right. But his older brothers were jealous of Joseph, and one day they sold him to some men who were going to Egypt. They let their father believe that Joseph had been killed by a wild animal.

While Joseph was in Egypt, Pharaoh had a dream about a coming famine. The Lord helped Joseph understand the dream. Then Pharaoh asked Joseph to help store food so there would be no famine in Egypt.

Later, when Joseph's brothers came to Egypt to buy food, Joseph was happy to see them and forgave them for being unkind to him. He asked them to bring their father and their families to live in Egypt. Imagine how happy Joseph's father was to see him again.

Moses Is Born

Many years later, a new pharaoh of Egypt was afraid the Israelites were becoming stronger than the Egyptians, so he made a law to kill all the Israelite baby boys.

To save her baby boy, one mother made a basket and put her newborn son in it. She floated the basket on the river and told her daughter, Miriam, to hide in the reeds and watch what would happen.

Pharaoh's daughter found the basket with the baby in it. She saved the baby and took care of him. She named him Moses, and the boy grew up a prince in Pharaoh's palace.

God Speaks to Moses

After Moses grew up, he left Egypt to live in the land of Midian. There the Lord spoke to Moses from a burning bush. The Israelites had become slaves, and God told Moses to tell Pharaoh to let the Israelites go. But Pharaoh said, "No!" Then the Lord sent plagues and sickness and death to the Egyptians. Finally, Pharaoh told Moses he could take the children of Israel and leave Egypt.

Crossing the Red Sea

Moses led the children of Israel out of Egypt. They crossed a desert and finally came to the Red Sea. Moses prayed, and the Lord parted the waters of the sea so the people could cross on dry ground. When Pharaoh's army tried to follow them and bring them back to Egypt, the sea closed up and drowned the soldiers. The children of Israel were safe, and they thanked the Lord for saving them from their enemies.

The Ten Commandments

One day the Lord led Moses to a high mountain called Sinai, where He gave Moses some special laws called the Ten Commandments.

The Ten Commandments taught the people to love and obey Heavenly Father, to love their parents, and to be honest and kind to one another. The Lord promised them that obeying the commandments would help them to be happy.

Joshua

After Moses died, the Lord made Joshua the leader of the children of Israel. Joshua led the people into the promised land. The people who were already living there were wicked. Joshua told the Israelites that before they entered the promised land, they needed to decide whether or not they would serve Heavenly Father. Joshua said that he and his family would serve the Lord. The Israelites also promised that they would obey Heavenly Father.

The Battle of Jericho

The Israelites had to conquer the promised land before they could live there. The first city they came to was Jericho. There were high walls around the city.

The Lord told Joshua to tell the people to march around Jericho every day for six days. Then on the seventh day they were to march around the city seven times and the priests were to blow their trumpets while everyone shouted. The people did as Joshua commanded, and the walls of Jericho fell down. The Israelites won the battle and were able to enter the promised land.

Jonah and the Whale

The Lord called Jonah on a mission to the wicked city of Nineveh, but Jonah was afraid to go. He decided to get on a boat and run away. There was a bad storm on the sea. Jonah realized the Lord was unhappy with him and told the sailors to throw him into the stormy sea.

God sent a large fish to swallow Jonah. After three days inside the fish, Jonah repented and promised to go on his mission. The big fish spit him out on the beach, and Jonah hurried to Nineveh. He taught the people the gospel, and they repented of their sins. Jonah had become a good missionary.

Hannah and Samuel

While Hannah was at the temple praying to have a child, she was promised by Eli the priest that God would answer her prayer. When her baby was born, Hannah was so thankful that she promised to give him back to the Lord. When Samuel was old enough, she took him to the temple to be a helper for Eli. One night the boy Samuel heard a voice calling him. He thought it was Eli, but it was the Lord, calling Samuel to be a prophet. Samuel listened to the Lord and obeyed Him.

The Lord Chooses a King for Israel

The Lord sent the prophet Samuel to call one of Jesse's sons to be the new king of Israel. All of Jesse's sons were strong and handsome, but the Lord told Samuel not to pay attention to how they looked on the outside. When Samuel looked at some of Jesse's sons, he knew the Lord had not chosen one of them. "Do you have any other sons?" he asked. Jesse sent for his youngest son, David, who was tending the sheep. When Samuel saw David, he knew the Lord had chosen the boy to be the king. David had a good heart and loved Heavenly Father.

David and Goliath

The Philistines were at war with the Israelites. The Philistines had a giant named Goliath in their army. Every day Goliath would shout, "Send someone to fight me!" No one dared to fight a giant. But when young David heard Goliath's challenge, David asked the king for permission to fight the giant. David told the king that the Lord had already helped him kill a lion and a bear that had tried to eat David's sheep. David did not have a sword or armor. The only weapon he had was a sling shot and five smooth stones. Because David had so much faith, the Lord helped him kill the giant Goliath and save the army of Israel.

Daniel in the Lions' Den

Daniel was King Darius's trusted helper. Some of the king's other helpers were jealous of Daniel and tricked the king into making a law that everyone must pray to the king instead of to God. These wicked men knew that Daniel prayed three times a day to Heavenly Father and that he would not pray to the king. They waited and watched until they found Daniel saying his prayers. Then they put Daniel into a den of lions. The king was sorry that he had made the law. He fasted and worried all night, hoping that his friend Daniel would be safe. In the morning, the king hurried to see what had happened to Daniel.

Daniel was safe. The Lord had sent an angel to protect Daniel from the hungry lions.

Queen Esther

Esther was a young Israelite woman who lived in Persia. The king of Persia chose Esther to be his queen because she was good and kind as well as beautiful. One of the king's helpers didn't like the Israelites. The king didn't know Queen Esther was an Israelite and was tricked by the wicked Haman into making a law to have the Israelites killed. Esther and all the Israelites fasted and prayed for three days, then Esther begged the king to spare her and her people. Haman was punished, and the Israelites thanked the Lord for Esther's courage and for saving them.

Elijah and the Widow

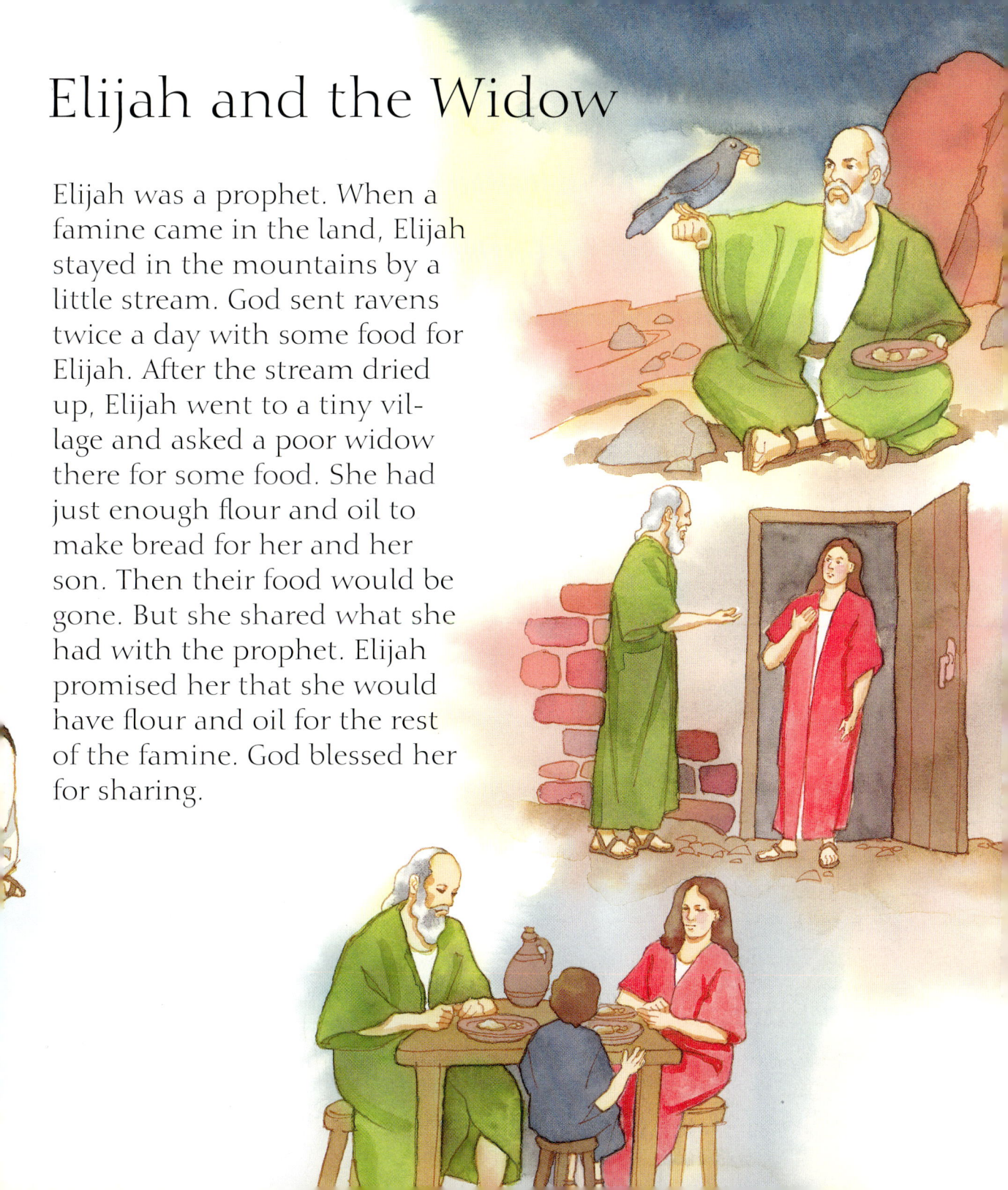

Elijah was a prophet. When a famine came in the land, Elijah stayed in the mountains by a little stream. God sent ravens twice a day with some food for Elijah. After the stream dried up, Elijah went to a tiny village and asked a poor widow there for some food. She had just enough flour and oil to make bread for her and her son. Then their food would be gone. But she shared what she had with the prophet. Elijah promised her that she would have flour and oil for the rest of the famine. God blessed her for sharing.

Naaman and Elisha

Naaman was a leader in the Syrian army. He was a good man, but he had a terrible skin disease called leprosy. A young Israelite girl, who was a maid in his house, told Naaman that Elisha the prophet could cure his leprosy. When Naaman went to visit Elisha, the prophet told him to wash seven times in the Jordan River. Naaman didn't think that would help and started to go home. But his friends said, "If the prophet had told you to do something hard, you would have done it, but you think this is too easy."

Naaman was sorry his faith had been so weak and obeyed Elisha. His leprosy was healed! He was blessed because he listened to the prophet.

Malachi

Malachi was the last Old Testament prophet. He promised that the Lord will open the windows of heaven and bless us if we will pay our tithing. Paying tithing shows Heavenly Father that we are thankful for our blessings and that we believe in Him.

Malachi also taught that the prophet Elijah would come in the last days to plant in the hearts of the children the promises made to the fathers, and that the hearts of the children would turn to their fathers. Elijah appeared to Joseph Smith in the Kirtland Temple and gave him the sealing power. Families who are sealed in the temple can be together forever.

My First NEW TESTAMENT Stories

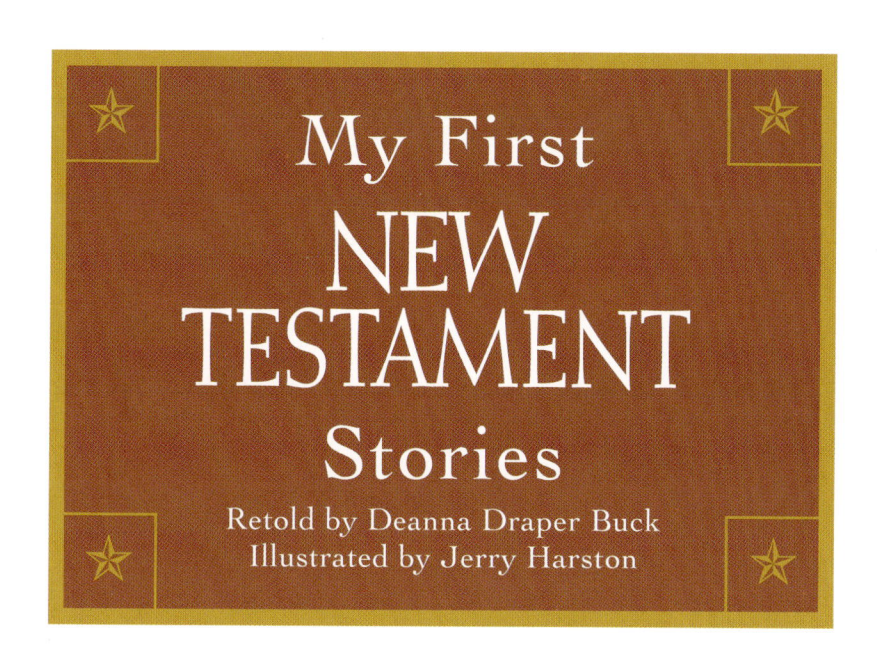

Retold by Deanna Draper Buck
Illustrated by Jerry Harston

Jesus Is Born

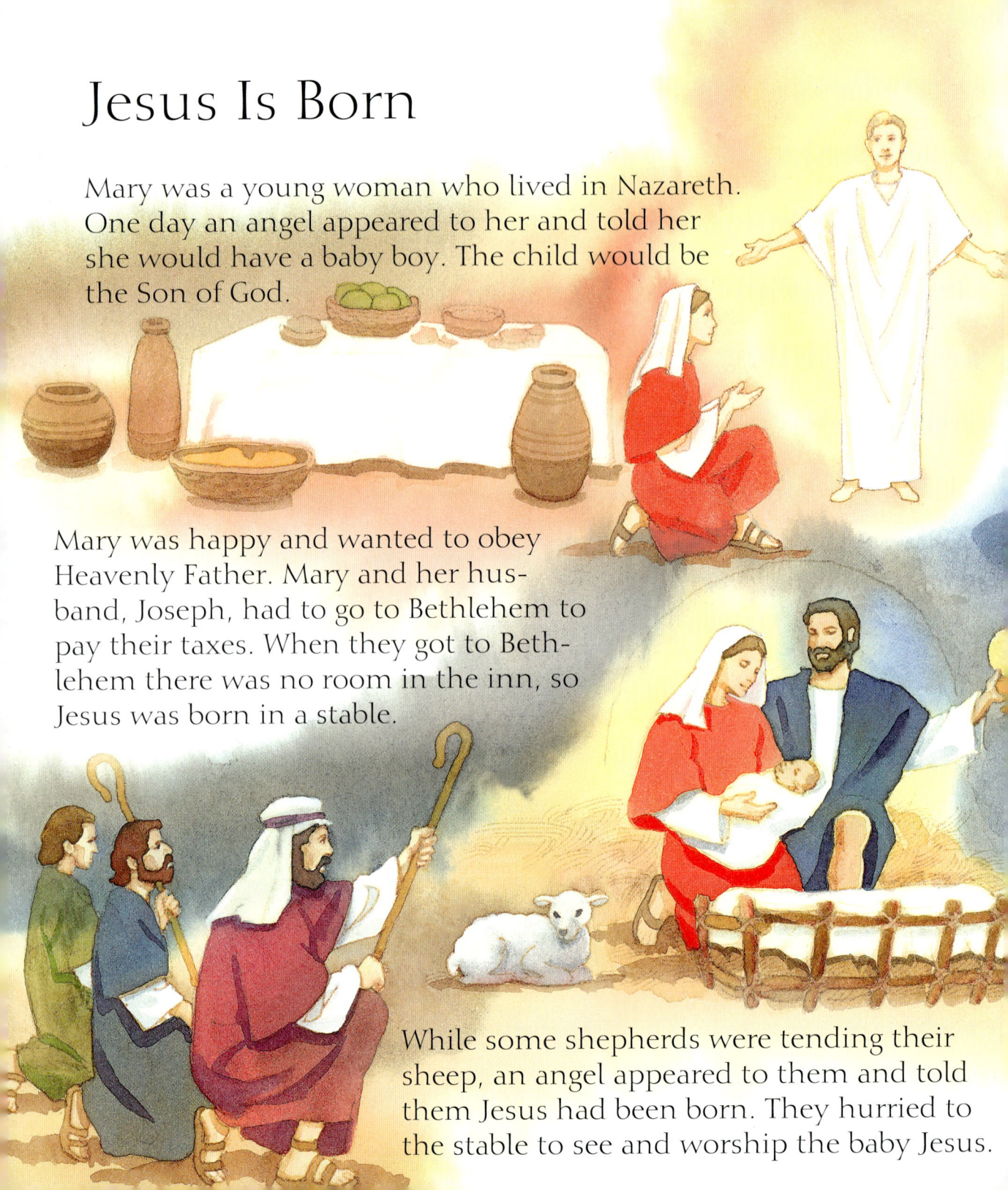

Mary was a young woman who lived in Nazareth. One day an angel appeared to her and told her she would have a baby boy. The child would be the Son of God.

Mary was happy and wanted to obey Heavenly Father. Mary and her husband, Joseph, had to go to Bethlehem to pay their taxes. When they got to Bethlehem there was no room in the inn, so Jesus was born in a stable.

While some shepherds were tending their sheep, an angel appeared to them and told them Jesus had been born. They hurried to the stable to see and worship the baby Jesus.

The Wise Men

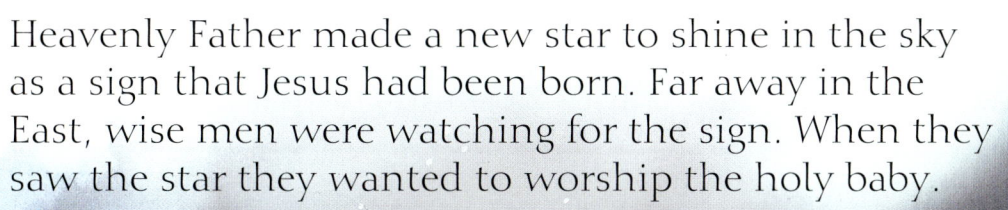

Heavenly Father made a new star to shine in the sky as a sign that Jesus had been born. Far away in the East, wise men were watching for the sign. When they saw the star they wanted to worship the holy baby.

They traveled far and brought precious gifts of gold, frankincense, and myrrh to Jesus. The Wise Men knew that Jesus was the Son of God and would be our Savior.

Jesus in the Temple

When Jesus was twelve years old, he went to Jerusalem with Joseph and Mary for the Feast of the Passover. When it was time to go home, Mary and Joseph couldn't find Jesus.

They looked and looked and finally found him in the temple with the rabbis and teachers. Jesus was teaching them and answering their questions. When Joseph and Mary told Jesus they had been worried, he said he was doing what Heavenly Father wanted him to do.

John the Baptist

John the Baptist was a prophet. He was chosen by Heavenly Father to prepare the people to listen to Jesus. John taught the people to repent and to keep the commandments. Many people believed John and wanted to obey Heavenly Father. After they repented, John baptized them in the Jordan River.

Jesus Is Baptized

Jesus came to John to be baptized. He told John that everyone needs to be baptized to show Heavenly Father they want to obey his commandments. After Jesus was baptized, by immersion, the Holy Ghost came down, like a dove, and rested on Jesus.

Then Heavenly Father spoke from heaven and said, "This is my beloved Son, in whom I am well pleased."

Disciples and Apostles

Jesus taught the people to be kind and to help each other. He healed the sick and did many other miracles. Many people believed Jesus and wanted to follow his teachings. These people were called disciples. Jesus chose twelve of his disciples to be apostles, and he gave them special priesthood authority. They could baptize and also perform miracles. The apostles knew that Jesus is the Son of God and would become the Savior of the world.

Peter, James, and John

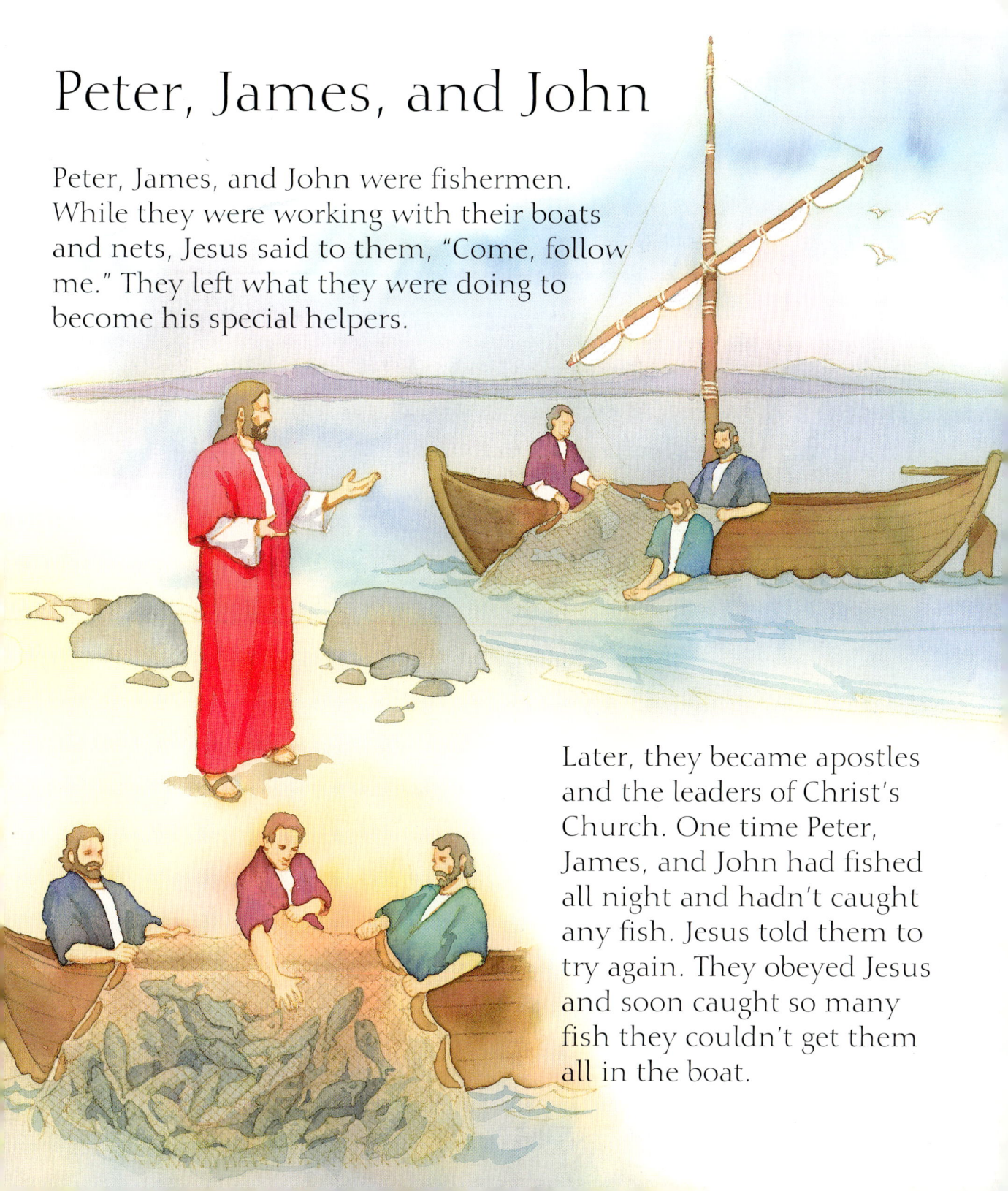

Peter, James, and John were fishermen. While they were working with their boats and nets, Jesus said to them, "Come, follow me." They left what they were doing to become his special helpers.

Later, they became apostles and the leaders of Christ's Church. One time Peter, James, and John had fished all night and hadn't caught any fish. Jesus told them to try again. They obeyed Jesus and soon caught so many fish they couldn't get them all in the boat.

The Sermon on the Mount

One day Jesus climbed a mountain. The people wanted to hear his teachings, and they followed him. He taught them that they should love and forgive everyone. That they should be kind and treat others the way they would like others to treat them. He said that if someone asks for help, we should do more than we are asked to do.

He also taught the people how to pray. He promised that doing these things will help us and others to be happy.

Jesus Performs Many Miracles

Jesus performed many miracles. He healed people who were sick or who couldn't walk or hear or see. Jesus even brought back to life some people who had died.

One day ten men who had a terrible disease called leprosy came to see Jesus. They asked to be healed. He blessed them and they got better.

They were all happy, but only one remembered to say thank you. Jesus taught us that we should always thank Heavenly Father for our blessings.

Feeding the Five Thousand

One day more than 5,000 people came to listen to Jesus. It was getting late and the people were hungry. But no one had brought any food except one boy who had five small loaves of bread and two small fishes.

Jesus said a blessing on the food, then broke it into pieces and had it passed to the large crowd. Everyone had all they wanted to eat, and there was even a lot of food left over. It was a miracle.

Calming the Sea

One time Jesus fell asleep while sailing in a small boat with his apostles. It was nighttime and a terrible storm arose on the sea. The apostles were afraid the boat would sink, so they woke up Jesus.

He spoke to the storm and said, "Peace, be still." The wind and the waves obeyed Jesus, and the sea became calm. Jesus and his apostles were able to get across the water safely.

Jesus Walks on the Water

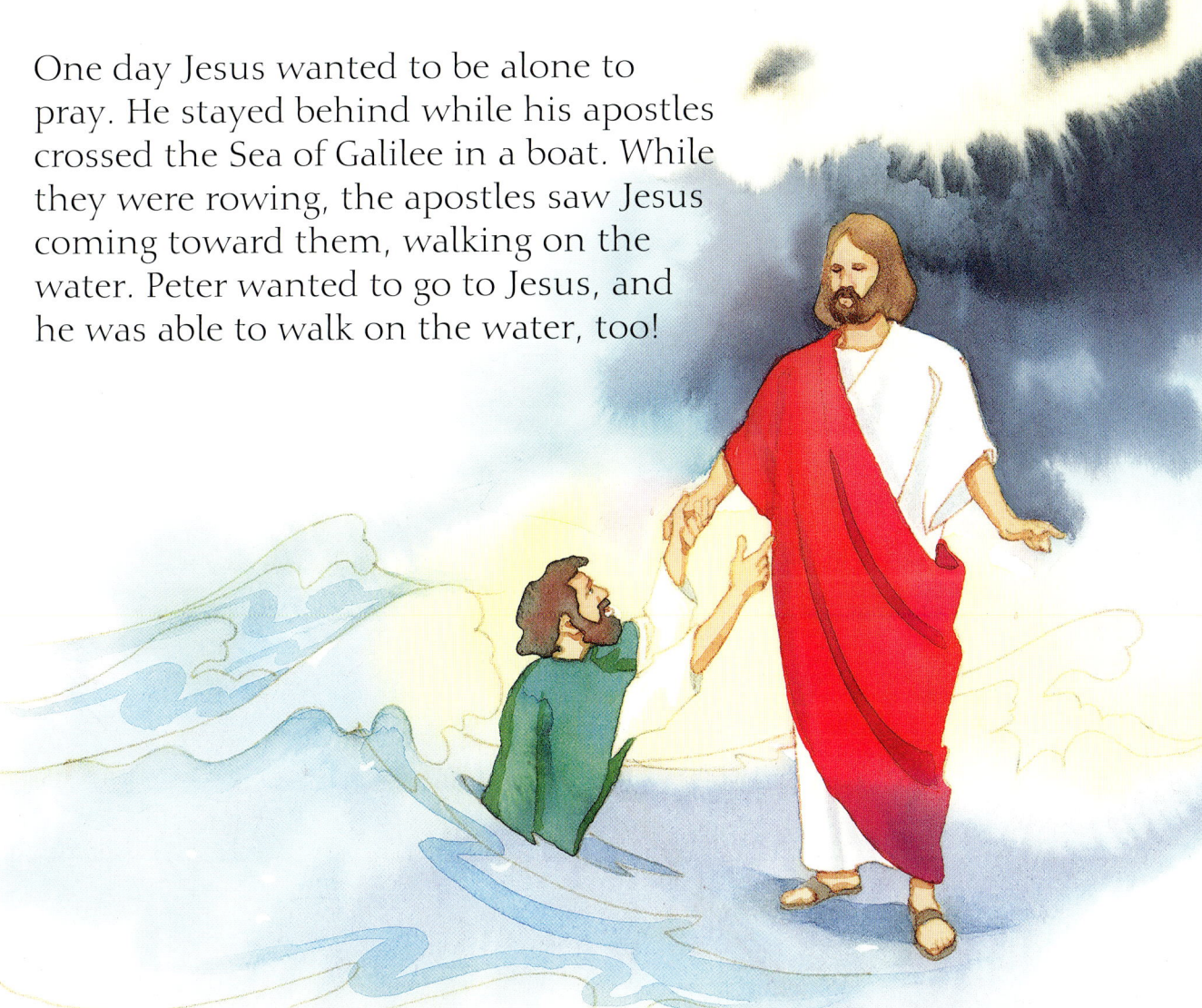

One day Jesus wanted to be alone to pray. He stayed behind while his apostles crossed the Sea of Galilee in a boat. While they were rowing, the apostles saw Jesus coming toward them, walking on the water. Peter wanted to go to Jesus, and he was able to walk on the water, too!

But when Peter looked down at the waves, he became afraid and lost his faith. As Peter began to sink, Jesus reached out his hand and caught him. Then Jesus and Peter walked back to the boat together.

Blessing the Children

Some mothers brought their children to Jesus to be blessed. His followers told the mothers that Jesus was too busy to bother with little children. But Jesus reached out for the children and held them in his arms and gave each of them a blessing.

Jesus told his disciples that we all need to be like innocent little children if we want to go to heaven.

The Lost Sheep

Jesus told his followers stories called parables. One of his stories was about a shepherd who had one hundred sheep. One day a lamb wandered off, so the shepherd left the other ninety-nine to go search for the little lost sheep. When he found it he carried it back to safety with the rest of his flock.

Jesus is the Good Shepherd, and we are his sheep. He loves all of us and watches over us. He wants all of us to be together with him in heaven.

The Good Samaritan

A man was walking along a road when some mean men beat and robbed him. The robbers left the injured man lying on the side of the road. All the people walking by pretended they didn't see the wounded man. But a man from Samaria stopped to help.

The kindly Samaritan cleaned and bandaged the man's cuts, then put the man on his donkey and took him to an inn. The good Samaritan gave the innkeeper some money to take care of the man.

Jesus taught that we are all neighbors. He wants us to be kind and helpful to each other.

The Prodigal Son

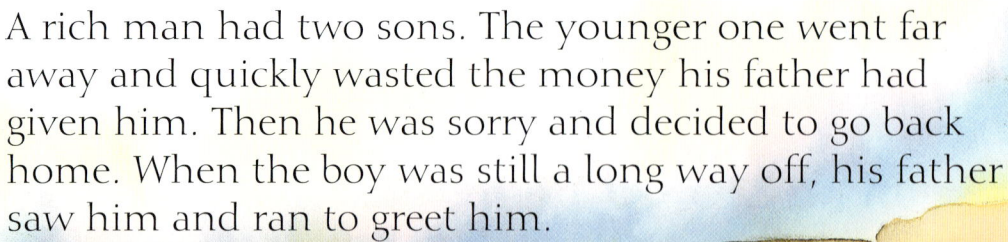

A rich man had two sons. The younger one went far away and quickly wasted the money his father had given him. Then he was sorry and decided to go back home. When the boy was still a long way off, his father saw him and ran to greet him.

The man was so happy to have his son come home that he gave a party. The oldest son was jealous and unhappy that he never got a party.

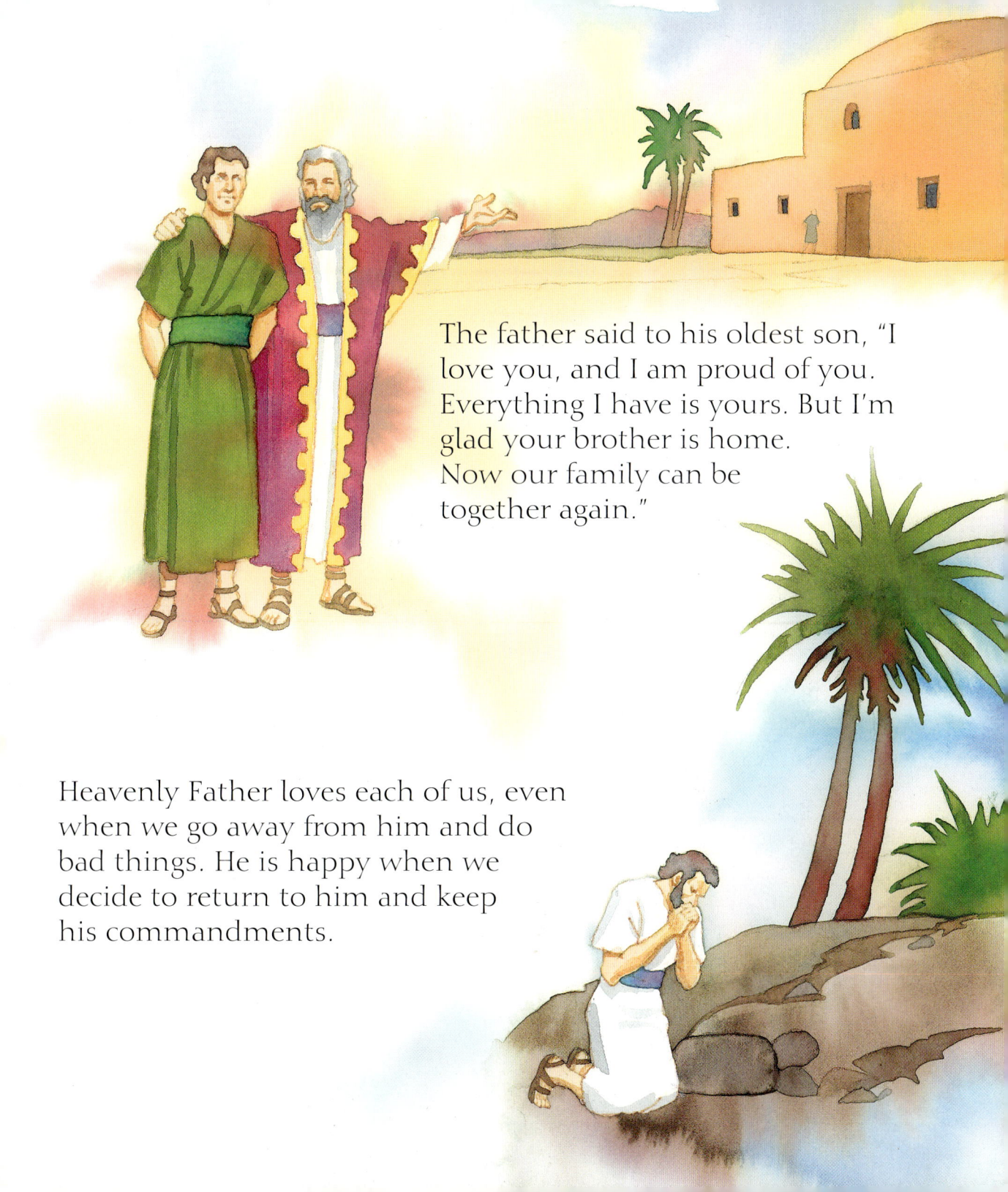

The father said to his oldest son, "I love you, and I am proud of you. Everything I have is yours. But I'm glad your brother is home. Now our family can be together again."

Heavenly Father loves each of us, even when we go away from him and do bad things. He is happy when we decide to return to him and keep his commandments.

Lazarus

Mary and Martha sent a message to Jesus that their brother, Lazarus, was sick. By the time Jesus arrived at their home, Mary and Martha were crying because Lazarus had already died and was buried. Because Jesus loved them, he cried too. Then they went to the tomb, and Jesus commanded Lazarus to come forth.

Lazarus obeyed Jesus. His spirit came back into his body, and he walked out of the tomb. Think how happy these people were.

Jesus used his power to bless those who believed in him.

Zacchaeus

Zacchaeus was a little man. When Jesus came to his town, Zacchaeus was too short to see over the crowd. So he ran ahead and climbed a tree so he could see Jesus when he passed by. Jesus looked up and said, "Zacchaeus, come down from the tree. I want to come to your house today."

Zacchaeus was surprised that Jesus knew he was in the tree. He was even more surprised that Jesus knew his name. Jesus sees all of us and knows each of our names. He loves everyone.

The Great Commandment

When Jesus was asked which commandment was the most important, he said it was to love Heavenly Father. He said the second most important commandment is to love our neighbors as ourselves.

He commanded us to love each other and showed his love for us by dying for us.

The Last Supper

Jesus knew that he would soon be killed, and he wanted to eat one last supper with his apostles. He taught them about the sacrament, and after they had eaten, Jesus washed his friends' feet. He told them he was going away and taught them to love each other. Then he prayed to Heavenly Father and asked him to bless the apostles. They finished their meeting by singing a hymn.

The Atonement

Jesus took his apostles with him to a garden called Gethsemane. He asked them to wait and pray for him while he prayed to his Father. He thought about all our sins and was very sad. He suffered for our sins, so we wouldn't have to. It was a very hard time for him, but he did it because he loves us.

This is called the Atonement. Because of it we can repent of our sins and return to live with Heavenly Father and Jesus after we die.

The Crucifixion

Wicked men were jealous of Jesus. They came to the Garden of Gethsemane and took Jesus. Then they had the Roman soldiers crucify him. After he died on the cross, Jesus' friends took his body and put it in a tomb.

The wicked men remembered that Jesus had said he would come alive again in three days. So they closed the tomb up with a heavy stone and had the Roman soldiers guard it.

The Resurrection

On Sunday morning, some women who were friends of Jesus went to the tomb. The stone in front of the tomb had been rolled away, and the Roman soldiers were gone. The tomb was empty!

An angel told the women the wonderful news. Jesus had been resurrected and was alive again!

Soon Jesus appeared to his apostles and others. The people who loved Jesus were happy that he was resurrected. Because of him, after we die we will all be resurrected and have our bodies again.

Jesus Teaches the Apostles

After Jesus was resurrected he stayed on earth for a while and taught his apostles how to lead his Church. He told them to go and teach the whole world about Heavenly Father's plan of happiness. Jesus said he was going to heaven but that he would come back to earth someday. Then he went to live with Heavenly Father.

After Jesus was gone, the apostles received the gift of the Holy Ghost. Peter, James, and John and the others worked their whole lives teaching about Heavenly Father and Jesus. They obeyed his commandment to love one another.

The Epistles of Paul

Saul was a mean man. He tried to destroy Jesus' Church. Jesus appeared to Saul in a bright light and told him to stop being wicked and start being good. The light was so bright that Saul went blind.

He went to Ananias, who healed him of his blindness and taught him the gospel.

Saul changed his name to Paul and became a great missionary. He was an apostle and wrote letters, called epistles, to the members of the Church. You can read those letters in the New Testament.

The Book of Revelation

John was one of Jesus' apostles. Jesus loved John and promised John that he wouldn't die until the end of the world. John had a vision of when Jesus would return to earth, and he wrote it down in a book called Revelation. When Jesus returns, the world will be beautiful, and all the people on earth will be good. There will be one thousand years of peace. It will be a wonderful time to be alive.

The book of Revelation is the last book in the New Testament.

My First BOOK OF MORMON Stories

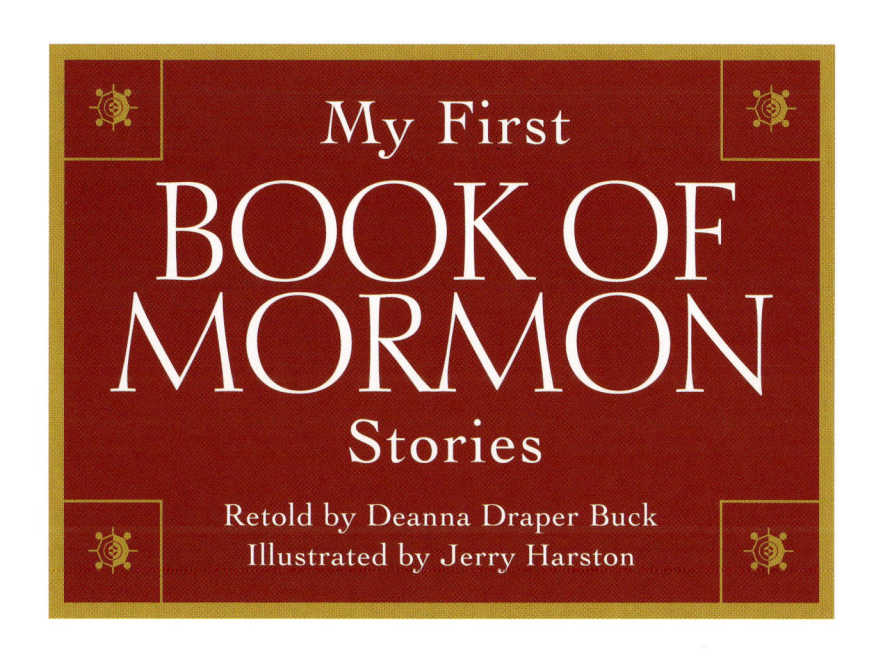

Retold by Deanna Draper Buck
Illustrated by Jerry Harston

Lehi Was a Prophet

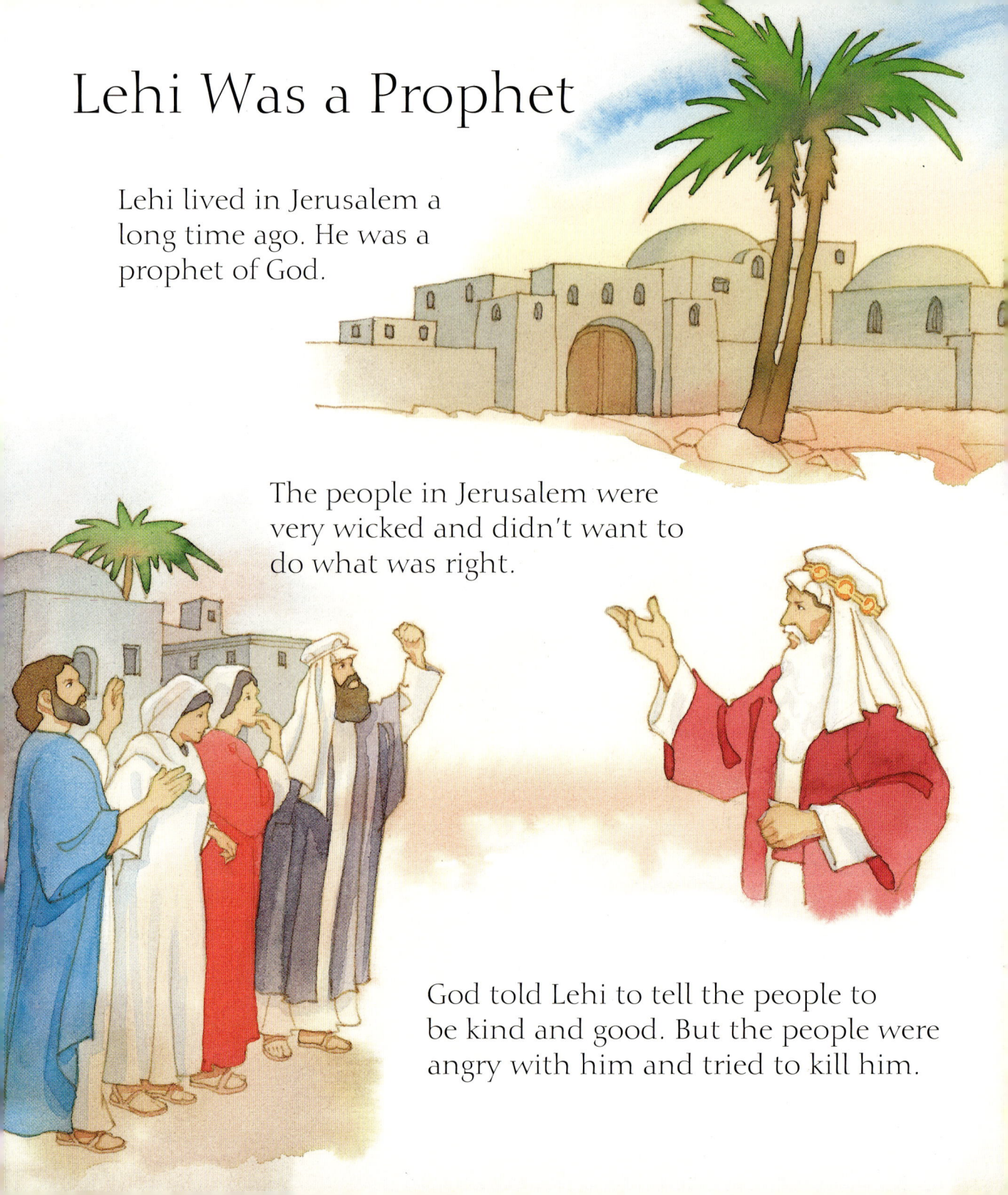

Lehi lived in Jerusalem a long time ago. He was a prophet of God.

The people in Jerusalem were very wicked and didn't want to do what was right.

God told Lehi to tell the people to be kind and good. But the people were angry with him and tried to kill him.

So God told Lehi to take his wife and children and leave Jerusalem.

God told them that he would lead them to a promised land.

Nephi Had Faith

Nephi was Lehi's youngest son. He knew that his father was a prophet of God. Nephi wanted to follow God and do what was right.

One day, after the family had left Jerusalem, Lehi asked his four sons to go back to Jerusalem to get the scriptures that were written on brass plates.

They would need to have the scriptures when they got to the Promised Land.

Nephi's brothers were afraid to go, so Nephi went alone.

Nephi knew that God would help him if he kept the commandments.

It was hard and dangerous to do, but Nephi was able, with God's help, to get the brass plates.

Lehi's Dream

The prophet Lehi had a dream of a beautiful tree with fruit that would make people happy. He saw a strait and narrow path and a rod of iron leading through a mist of darkness to the tree. By holding onto the iron rod people were able to come to the tree.

People in a large building were laughing at those who were eating the fruit. Lehi ate the fruit and asked his family to join him. Sariah, Sam, and Nephi came, but Laman and Lemuel would not. Lehi was sad that Laman and Lemuel would not partake of the fruit; he wanted his whole family to be together.

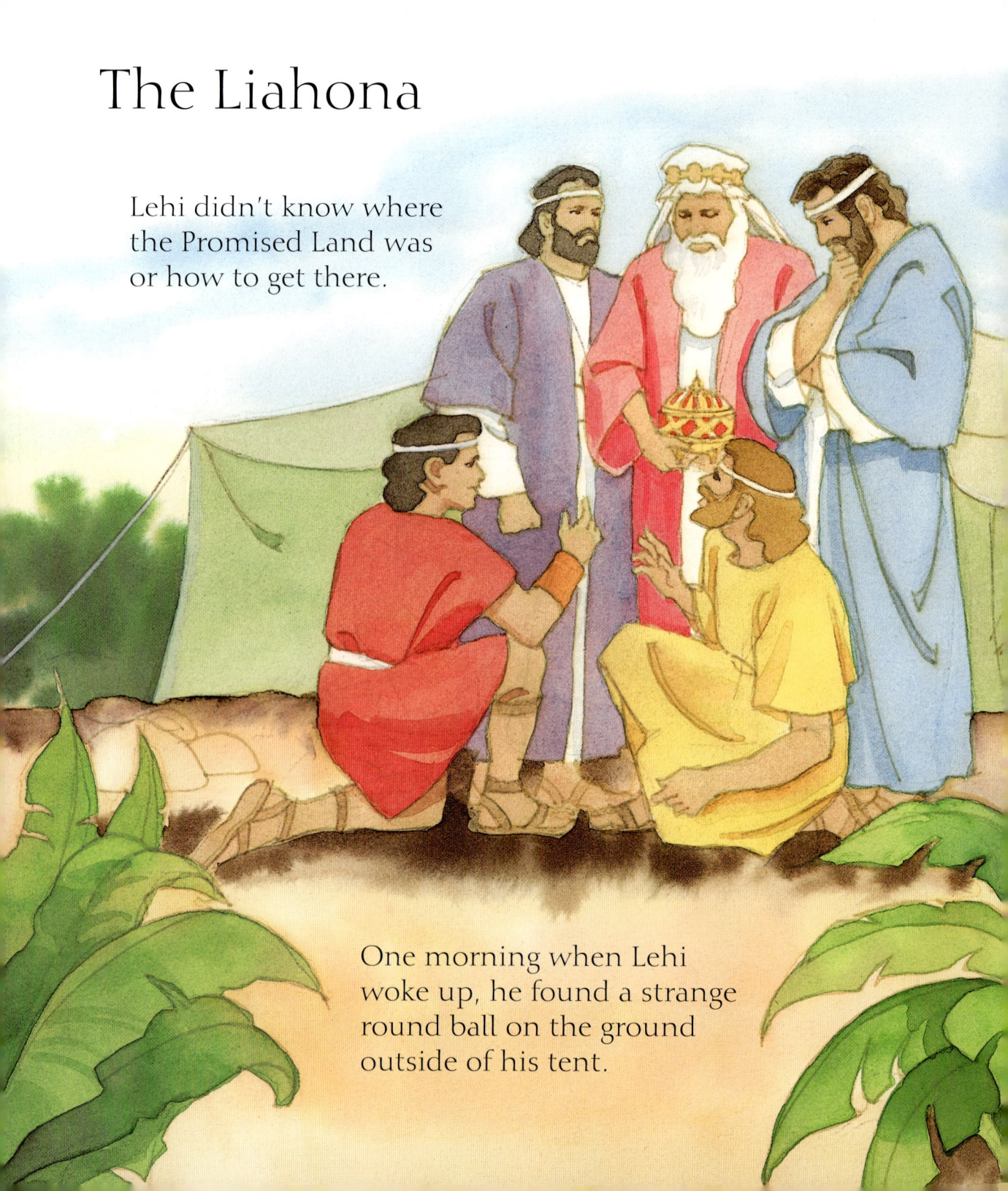

The Liahona

Lehi didn't know where the Promised Land was or how to get there.

One morning when Lehi woke up, he found a strange round ball on the ground outside of his tent.

It was the Liahona. It acted like a compass and pointed where to go. But the Liahona only worked when everyone obeyed God.

The Liahona showed Lehi's family and friends the way to the Promised Land.

Nephi and the Broken Bow

When Lehi's family left Jerusalem they took their bows and arrows so they could hunt for food. Nephi's strong steel bow broke, and his brothers' bows had lost their spring and didn't work.

Everyone was hungry and started to complain, even Lehi. Nephi didn't complain, instead he made a new wooden bow and arrow. Then he asked his father where he should go hunting.

Lehi was sorry that he had complained and asked the Lord where to send Nephi to hunt.

The Lord answered his prayer. Nephi brought back many wild beasts to feed their families. Everyone was happy and thanked Heavenly Father for helping them.

Nephi Builds a Ship

After a long time in the wilderness, Lehi's group came to the sea. God told Nephi to build a ship big enough to carry the people across the sea.

Nephi's brothers thought that he couldn't build a ship. They made fun of him.

But God told Nephi how to build the ship and showed him where to find wood and how to make the tools he needed.

He built a sturdy ship, and the whole family sailed safely to a special land kept secret by Heavenly Father.

A Storm at Sea

While Lehi's family was sailing to the Promised Land, Laman and Lemuel and their wives began being disobedient. When Nephi asked them to keep the commandments, they were angry with him and tied him up.

The Liahona quit working and a terrible storm came. No matter what anyone said, Laman and Lemuel would not untie Nephi.

On the fourth day Laman and Lemuel were afraid that the ship would sink so they finally set Nephi free. The Liahona began working again and after Nephi prayed the storm stopped. With the Lord's help, Nephi was able to steer the ship safely to the Promised Land.

Jacob and Sherem

Jacob was a prophet who saw that Jesus would be born and be our Savior. A wicked man named Sherem was telling the Nephites that Jesus was only a story and they shouldn't believe Jacob. Sherem said that he would not believe in Jesus unless God sent him a sign. When Jacob prayed God sent a sign to Sherem.

Sherem fell to the ground and became very sick. Right before he died he asked all of the Nephites to listen to him. He told them that he was sorry and was wrong to have believed the devil's lies. The people followed Jacob and believed that Jesus was our Savior.

Enos

Enos was born in the Promised Land. His father was Nephi's younger brother Jacob.

One day Enos was hunting. He thought about the things his father had taught him about Jesus.

He knelt down and prayed. He prayed all day long. He asked Heavenly Father to forgive him.

He prayed for his friends and also for his enemies and asked God to bless them. Enos had learned to love everyone, even those who did not love him.

King Benjamin

Benjamin was a good king. He loved his people and wanted to teach them to be kind. He built a tall tower to stand on while he talked to them.

He taught them to love and to help each other. He told the parents that they should teach their children not to fight.

He told his people that when they helped each other, it was the same as helping God.

Abinadi

Later, the Nephites had another king. His name was Noah, and he was a wicked man who did not obey Heavenly Father.

Abinadi was a prophet of God. He came to King Noah and taught him and his wicked priests about Jesus.

Abinadi was very brave, and he told Noah that kings and leaders should help their people to be good.

This made King Noah angry, and he had his guards kill Abinadi.

Alma

Alma was one of the priests of King Noah. Alma believed the teachings of Abinadi and left King Noah to go and teach the people the things that Abinadi taught.

Alma told the people to be kind and to share and to help each other. Some of the people were happy to learn about Jesus.

They wanted to be baptized so that they could be members of Christ's Church.

Alma and His People Escape

Alma and his followers left the land of Nephi so that they could worship God. But the Lamanite soldiers found Alma's people and captured them.

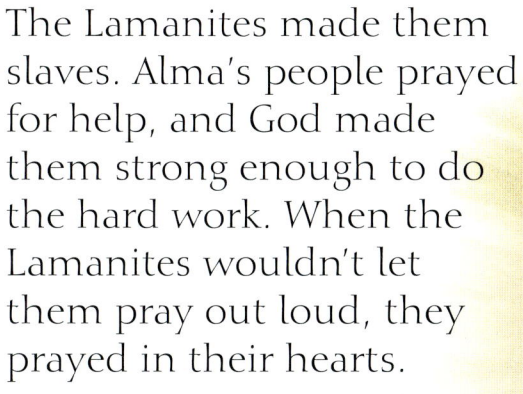

The Lamanites made them slaves. Alma's people prayed for help, and God made them strong enough to do the hard work. When the Lamanites wouldn't let them pray out loud, they prayed in their hearts.

Heavenly Father made the guards fall asleep, and the people of Alma were able to escape and go to the land of Zarahemla to be with the rest of the Nephites.

Alma the Younger and the Sons of King Mosiah

Alma had a son who was also named Alma. He was called Alma the Younger.

His best friends were the four sons of King Mosiah.

These five boys didn't want to obey their parents or Heavenly Father. They caused a lot of trouble.

Their parents prayed for them, and God sent an angel to talk with the boys.

The angel told them that what they were doing was wrong.

The boys were sorry for being bad. They repented and later became great missionaries.

Alma the Younger and Amulek

As a missionary, Alma the Younger tried to teach the people of Ammonihah about Jesus. When they would not listen to him, he was sad and left the city. An angel stopped him and told him to return to the city. Alma had been fasting for many days and was very hungry.

When he got back to the city he asked a man for some food. The man was Amulek. Amulek said that an angel had already told him about Alma. He welcomed Alma into his home. Alma taught him the gospel, and Amulek became his missionary companion.

Zeezrom

Alma taught the people in Ammonihah about the Savior. A wicked man named Zeezrom tried to trick Alma into saying things that were not true. Alma had the Spirit of the Lord, so he could not be tricked. Zeezrom offered Alma a lot of money if he would turn against God.

Alma and his companion Amulek spoke with the power of God and finally Zeezrom believed them. Zeezrom was sorry and tried to get the other people to believe Alma. But the people were angry with him. They threw rocks at him and chased Zeezrom away.

Zeezrom worried about his sins and became very sick. Alma gave him a blessing, and when Zeezrom got better, Alma baptized him. After his baptism, Zeezrom also became a missionary.

Alma and Amulek in Prison

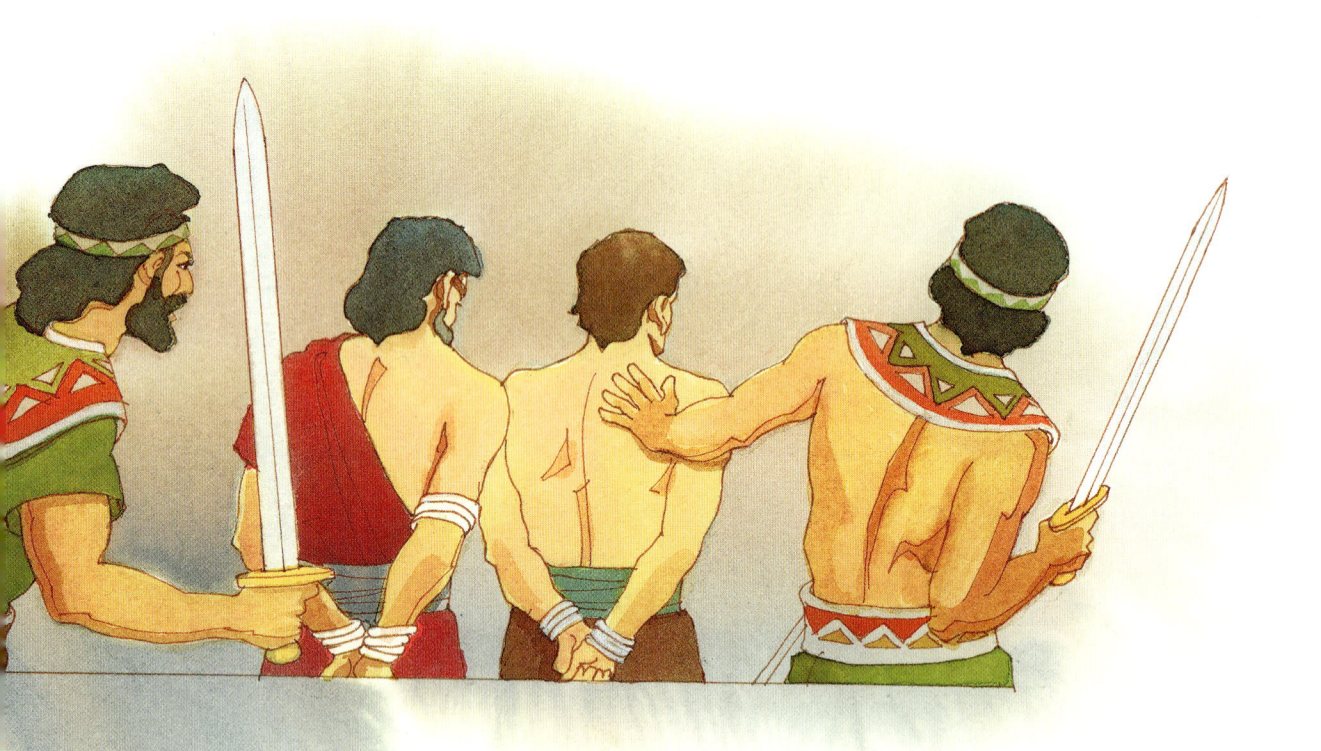

The people of Ammonihah did not want to learn about Jesus. Even though Alma and Amulek had done nothing wrong they were put in prison. Wicked men came to the prison every day to make fun of them and hit them, but Alma and Amulek never said a word in reply. After many days, when Alma and Amulek were very weak and tired, they prayed that the Lord would give them strength to break the cords that tied them.

The Lord made it possible for them to break the strong cords. When the wicked men saw that the prisoners were free, they became frightened and began to run. As they ran the ground shook and the prison walls fell down, killing all of the wicked men. God protected Alma and Amulek, who came out of the prison without being hurt.

Ammon and King Lamoni

Ammon was one of the sons of King Mosiah. He went on a mission to the Lamanites. He became a servant of a Lamanite king named Lamoni and saved the king's sheep from robbers.

The king asked Ammon why he was so strong and good, and Ammon taught King Lamoni about the Savior. King Lamoni believed Ammon and prayed to Heavenly Father.

After his prayer he fell to the ground. His servants placed the king on his bed where he lay for two days. Ammon knew that Lamoni was being taught by the Spirit of the Lord.

Some of Lamoni's servants thought he was dead and should be buried, but the queen thought her husband was alive. Ammon told the queen that Lamoni was alive and would wake up in the morning.

On the third day King Lamoni woke up and rose out of bed. He told the queen that the teachings of Ammon were true. The queen and all of their servants were converted to the Lord.

King Lamoni's Father

The Lord told Ammon that his brothers were in prison in the land of Middoni. Ammon wanted to save them, and Lamoni offered to go with him. Lamoni was friends with the king of Middoni. On their way to Middoni they met King Lamoni's father who was king of all the Lamanite lands. He was angry that his son was a friend of a Nephite and he tried to kill Ammon.

Ammon fought with the king and wounded him. Ammon told the king that he would kill him unless he helped free his brothers from prison and would not be angry with Lamoni.

The king was surprised that a Nephite loved his son. He agreed to do as Ammon asked, and then he invited Ammon and his brothers to come to his kingdom and teach him about Jesus.

Lamoni's Father's Conversion

King Lamoni's father also wanted to learn about Heavenly Father. Ammon's brother Aaron went to teach him. Aaron taught the king about the creation of the earth and about Adam and Eve and said that Jesus would come to the earth and be our Savior. Lamoni's father listened to all that Aaron taught him, then he humbly prayed and said, "Aaron has said that there is a God and if you are God, I will give away all of my sins to know thee."

God answered his prayer and Lamoni's father learned that there really is a Father in Heaven who loves and helps us.

The king then made a law that the missionaries could go in peace and teach his whole kingdom about Jesus. Many Lamanites learned to love the Savior and were baptized and lived in peace with the Nephites.

The People of Ammon

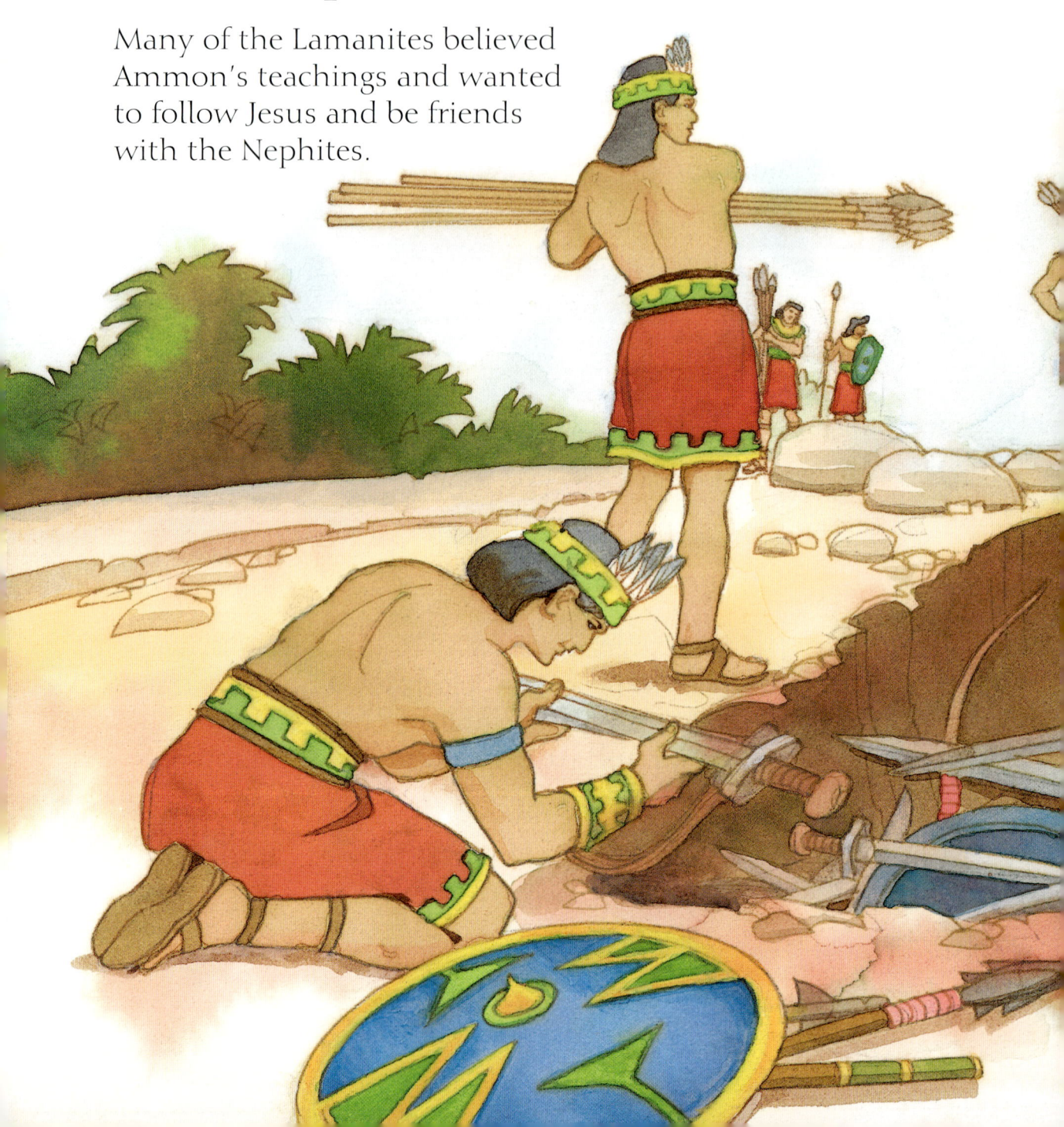

Many of the Lamanites believed Ammon's teachings and wanted to follow Jesus and be friends with the Nephites.

They learned that they should share and not fight anymore.

They buried their swords and bows and arrows in the ground and promised to never fight again.

To be safe, they moved into the Nephite lands, where they lived in peace for many years.

The Testimony of Christ Is Like a Seed

Alma was a good missionary and a powerful teacher. He loved people and taught the Zoramites that everyone needs to have faith in Jesus Christ.

He compared faith to a seed.

He said if you have a little seed and you plant it in good soil and give it water and sunshine it will grow into a tree.

Alma explained that even a small testimony of Christ can grow if we take care of it by praying,

reading the scriptures, listening to the prophets, and trying to do what is right. That tiny belief will grow, and we will have a strong testimony of Jesus.

Amulek Teaches the People to Pray

The poor people had worked hard to build the Zoramite churches but because they didn't have nice clothes to wear the rich people would not allow them to go into the church. The poor people thought that they could not pray unless they were inside the church. Amulek taught them that they could pray anywhere and that they should pray about everything that is important to them.

They should pray for their families and their work and for God to help them have more faith. Amulek reminded the people to pray for the poor. He told them that when they couldn't pray out loud, they should pray in their hearts.

Amulek also said that when we say our prayers, Heavenly Father helps us to be good and want to keep his commandments.

Captain Moroni and the Title of Liberty

Moroni was chosen to be the leader of the Nephite armies even though he was still a young man. He loved the Lord and he loved liberty. When Moroni found out that a wicked man named Amalickiah wanted to be the king and take away the freedoms of the people, Moroni was angry.

He tore his coat and wrote on it, "In memory of our God, our religion, and freedom, and our peace, our wives, and our children." He called it the "title of liberty" and fastened it onto a pole.

He put on his battle armor and went to every city. When the people read his title of liberty they put on their battle armor and joined him. They promised to obey God and fight to protect their families and their freedoms.

The Army of Helaman

Many of the Lamanites did not believe Ammon when he taught them about God, so they still wanted to fight the Nephites.

The Nephite soldiers needed more help. The grown-up boys of the good Lamanites said that they would help.

They were only babies when their parents promised never to fight again, so these young men had not made that promise.

They asked the prophet Helaman to be their leader. They were not afraid to fight even though they were young.

Their mothers had taught them to trust Jesus and promised them that if they would do what was right, God would protect them.

Nephi and Lehi

Nephi and Lehi were sons of the prophet Helaman. Nephi and Lehi were given their names by their father so that they would always remember to be like the prophets. They went on a mission to the Lamanites and converted thousands of them to the gospel.

They hadn't done anything wrong, but an army of Lamanites put them in prison. The men of the town went into the prison planning to kill Nephi and Lehi.

When they got there, they saw that Nephi and Lehi were surrounded by fire. The fire didn't hurt Nephi or Lehi. Then the wicked men heard a voice from heaven that told them to repent.

They repented and the fire surrounded them too. They believed the teachings of Nephi and Lehi and taught their friends about Jesus.

Samuel the Lamanite

Samuel was a Lamanite and a prophet. He went to the Nephites and told them that Jesus was going to be born in just five more years.

He said that when Jesus was to be born, a new star would appear in the sky and there would be a day and a night and a day when it wouldn't get dark.

Some of the people believed him and were very happy that Jesus would soon be born.

But some people were angry with Samuel and tried to kill him. Heavenly Father protected Samuel so that their arrows could not hit him.

Jesus Is Born

Five years after Samuel taught the people from the city wall, the star that he promised appeared in the sky. Other great lights also appeared.

When the sun went down that night, it didn't get dark. That was how the people knew that Jesus had been born far across the sea in the land of Jerusalem.

Many people were very happy and hoped that Jesus would also come to the Promised Land to visit them.

Jesus Is Crucified

Thirty-three years after the signs of Jesus' birth were given, many people had forgotten about Jesus and were being cruel and wicked.

They had become selfish and would not share with or help other people.

The people in Jerusalem, far across the sea, were being wicked too. They were so wicked that they crucified Jesus.

When Jesus died, there were terrible storms and earthquakes in the Promised Land.

It was totally dark for three days. Houses and cities were destroyed, and the people were frightened. Many of them died.

Jesus Visits the Promised Land

After the three days of darkness, Jesus was resurrected and came alive again in Jerusalem.

He visited his friends there. He told them that he had "other sheep" to visit. Those "other sheep" were the people in the Promised Land.

When Jesus came to the Promised Land, it made the people very happy. He showed himself to them and taught them his gospel.

Jesus loved the little children and blessed them one by one. And angels came and also blessed the children.

Everyone was happy and promised to be kind and to love and help each other.

The Three Nephites

Jesus chose twelve men to be his disciples; they would lead the church after he was gone. Just before Jesus went back to heaven he asked his disciples what they would like.

Nine of his disciples said that they wanted to be with him in heaven as soon as their work was done on earth. The other three wanted to continue living so they could teach people about Jesus and help them do what is right.

Jesus changed their bodies so that they would never die. When Jesus returns to earth, they will finish their missions and go to heaven.

Mormon

For the next two hundred years the people remembered Jesus and his teachings. They were happy and lived in peace. Later they became selfish and began to fight.

When Mormon became the leader of the people, he taught them to be good, but the people said no!

Mormon had been given all the books of the whole land. He read the books and then wrote the most important parts on a new set of golden plates.

He wrote about Lehi and Nephi and about Alma and Abinadi. He especially wrote about Jesus and how much Jesus loves us.

Then he gave the golden plates to his son, Moroni, and told him to take good care of them and keep them safe.

The Jaredites

Long, long ago, after Noah and his family and all of the animals got off the ark, the people started to build a tall tower.

They hoped it would be tall enough to reach to heaven. This made Heavenly Father unhappy with them, and he changed their language so they could not understand each other.

A man named Jared lived at this time. Jared and his family prayed to be able to still understand each other.

They were good people, and Heavenly Father told them he would lead them to a promised land. They traveled for many days. Finally they came to the sea.

Shining Stones

Jared had a brother who was a very good man. God showed Jared's brother how to build some boats so that the Jaredites could cross the ocean.

The boats had no windows, and it was dark inside of them.

The people didn't want to cross the ocean in the dark, so the Brother of Jared made sixteen clear stones and asked God to make them shine.

God touched the stones with his finger and made them glow. The Jaredites were able to travel to the Promised Land in the lighted boats.

Moroni

In one last great battle, the Lamanites killed Mormon and all the other Nephites, except Mormon's son, Moroni.

Moroni took the golden plates that he and his father had written on and buried them in a hill called Cumorah.

Mormon and Moroni were the last prophets of the Nephite People.

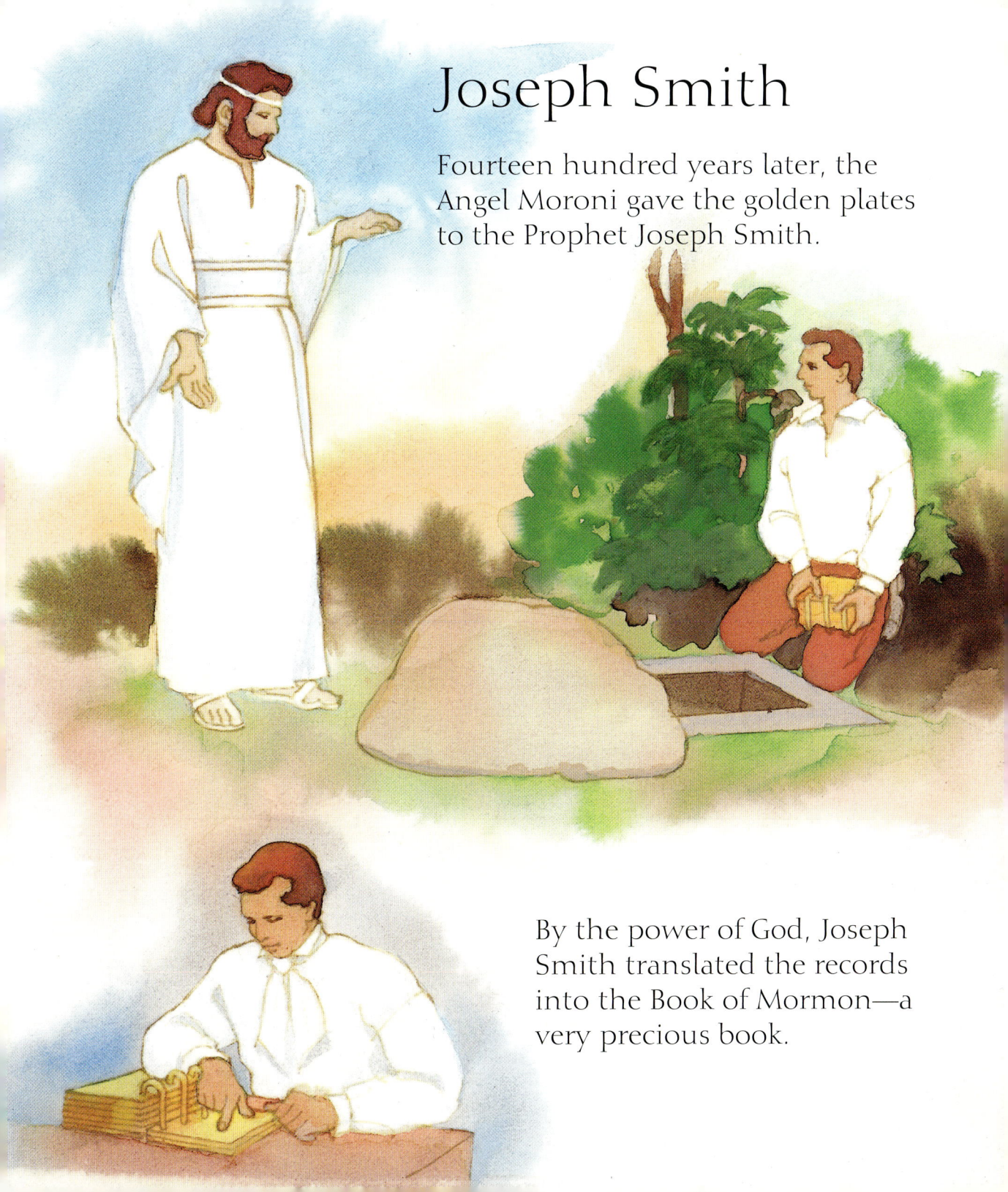

Joseph Smith

Fourteen hundred years later, the Angel Moroni gave the golden plates to the Prophet Joseph Smith.

By the power of God, Joseph Smith translated the records into the Book of Mormon—a very precious book.

My First CHURCH HISTORY Stories

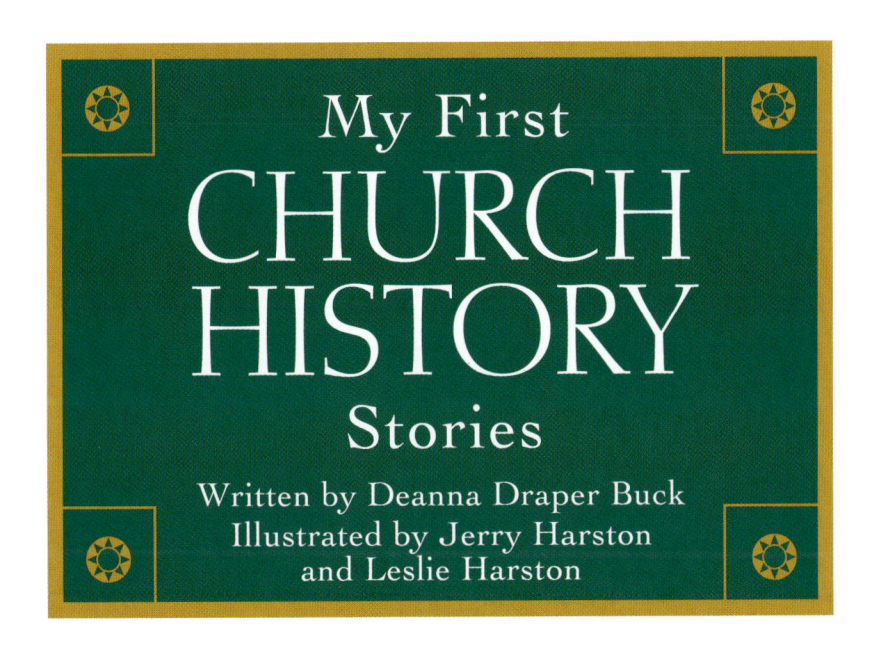

Written by Deanna Draper Buck
Illustrated by Jerry Harston
and Leslie Harston

Joseph Smith and the First Vision

Joseph Smith was our first prophet. When he was a boy he wondered which church he should join.

One beautiful spring morning he went into the woods near his home to pray, to ask Heavenly Father which church was right.

In answer to his prayer, he saw a vision of Heavenly Father and Jesus.

Joseph was told by Jesus not to join any church.

The Angel Moroni and the Book of Mormon

Three years later, an angel named Moroni came to Joseph Smith and told him about some gold plates buried in the Hill Cumorah.

Moroni visited Joseph every year and taught him the things he should do. After four years, Joseph was given the gold plates.

With Heavenly Father's help, Joseph was able to read the strange writing on the plates.

After Joseph translated the writings, they were printed in a book called the Book of Mormon.

The Book of Mormon tells us about Jesus and His teachings.

Many people have read the Book of Mormon. They know it is the word of God and follow its teachings.

The Priesthood

One day, Joseph Smith and his friend Oliver Cowdery were praying together. An angel named John appeared to them. It was John the Baptist, who had baptized Jesus.

The angel put his hands on the heads of Joseph and Oliver. He gave them the Aaronic Priesthood. Now they had the authority to baptize.

Later, Peter, James, and John appeared to Joseph and Oliver. They were Jesus' apostles, and they gave Joseph and Oliver the Melchizedek Priesthood.

The Church Is Organized

On April 6, 1830, The Church of Jesus Christ of Latter-day Saints was organized.

That first meeting was held in a small cabin in Fayette, New York. There were only six members at that time, but the Church soon began to grow.

The Kirtland Temple

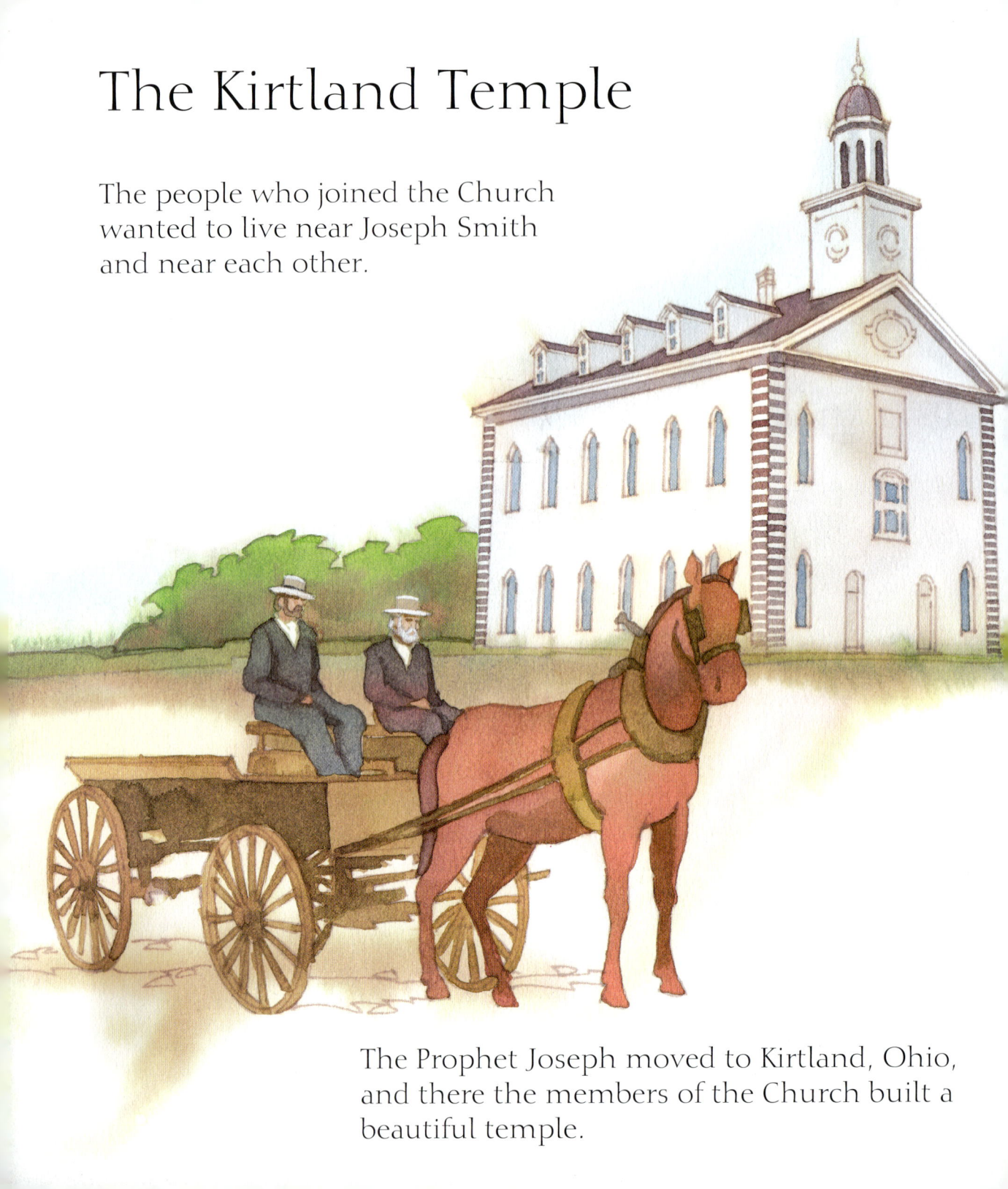

The people who joined the Church wanted to live near Joseph Smith and near each other.

The Prophet Joseph moved to Kirtland, Ohio, and there the members of the Church built a beautiful temple.

When the temple was dedicated, Jesus appeared in the temple and so did many angels.

Moses and Elias and Elijah gave instructions and authority to Joseph Smith.

Many people saw angels during the dedication of the Kirtland Temple. Everyone was happy and felt God's love.

The Gathering

Missionaries were sent to many lands to tell the people about Jesus and about the Book of Mormon and the new church.

A lot of people believed the missionaries. After they were baptized, the new members wanted to come to America to live near other members of the Church.

Some of the people went to live in Kirtland, Ohio. Others moved to Missouri.

Persecution

In Missouri, the members of the Church worked hard to build nice homes and farms.

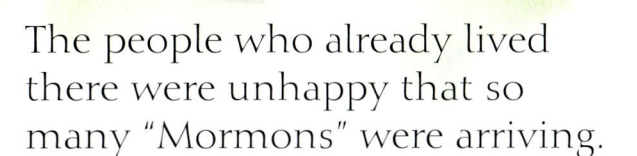

The people who already lived there were unhappy that so many "Mormons" were arriving.

They were afraid the Mormons would become too powerful. Some mean men put Joseph Smith in jail and told the members of the Church to leave the state.

Angry mobs burned some of the Mormons' houses and farms and even killed some members of the Church. Brigham Young and Heber C. Kimball led the Church members from Missouri to Illinois.

The Courage of Two Young Girls

The Lord spoke often to the Prophet Joseph Smith and taught him many things.

Joseph wanted these teachings and commandments to be written in a book so that everyone could read them.

While the Book of Commandments was being printed, a mob of angry men broke into the printing office and threw the unbound pages of the book into the street.

Two young Latter-day Saint girls, sisters Caroline and Mary Elizabeth Rollins, saw the pages lying on the ground and quickly gathered them up in their arms.

Running from the men who chased them, the two sisters hid in a field of tall cornstalks. Though they hunted all around them, the men could not find the girls.

The pages they saved were collected into a book called the Book of Commandments. Later, the book was called the Doctrine and Covenants.

A Miracle of Healing

Alma Smith was a seven-year-old boy who lived in the Mormon town of Haun's Mill, Missouri.

One day a mob of angry, mean men came to Haun's Mill.

They shot and killed many of the Mormon men and boys. They shot Alma in the hip, blowing the bone away. There weren't any doctors to take him to, and his mother didn't know what to do to help him.

But she had faith that because Heavenly Father made our bodies, He could make a new hipbone for Alma.

After she prayed, she knew what she should do. She washed the wound and then packed it with a mixture of water and ground-up tree root.

Alma had to lie in bed on his stomach for five weeks, until his hip was all better.

After that he was able to walk and run and play. He didn't even have a limp.

Alma and his mother thanked Heavenly Father for the miracle that had healed his hip.

The Whittling, Whistling Brigade

When Joseph Smith got out of jail, he also went to Illinois.

There the Saints built a beautiful city they named Nauvoo.

They built another temple and for a time were safe and happy.

Sometimes the enemies of the Church would come to Nauvoo to cause trouble. Joseph Smith asked some young men to follow the troublemakers.

The boys would whittle on sticks with their pocketknives and whistle while they followed them.

Soon the troublemakers would give up and get in a boat and leave Nauvoo. These boys were members of the Whittling, Whistling Brigade.

The Martyrdom

Trouble continued for the Saints. Angry men put Joseph Smith in jail again.

On a hot day in June 1844, a mob came to the jail in Carthage, Illinois, and killed Joseph and his brother Hyrum.

The Saints were very sad that their prophet was dead.

Brigham Young

The enemies of the Church thought that now the Church would die. They were wrong! This is the true church and cannot be stopped by anything.

The Saints didn't know who their new leader should be. Brigham Young was the senior Apostle.

When Brigham Young spoke at a meeting, many people said that he looked and sounded like Joseph Smith. Then the Saints knew Jesus had chosen "Brother Brigham" to be the next prophet.

Leaving Nauvoo

More and more people were baptized and moved to Nauvoo. The enemies of the Church became very angry.

They made the Mormons leave their beautiful homes and farms and move from Nauvoo.

It was wintertime, and it was so cold that the Mississippi River froze. The Saints crossed the river by driving their heavy wagons across the ice.

The Pioneers

The members of the Church needed a new place to live. The Saints became pioneers, and Brigham Young led them across the plains to the Salt Lake Valley.

It took three months to make the trip in a covered wagon. It was hard to be a pioneer, but the people helped each other, and they danced and sang around their campfires to make the long trip more fun.

When Brigham Young first saw the Salt Lake Valley, he said, "This is the right place." It was July 24, 1847.

Pioneer Children

Many children crossed the plains. Two of those children were Marie and Andrew. They were born in Denmark, and their father had died.

The two children were being raised by their mother and grandfather, who joined the Church and wanted to go to Utah.

When they arrived in America, the children's mother drove a covered wagon pulled by oxen, but Marie and Andrew and their grandpa walked all the way to Utah.

Every morning their grandfather would tie a small sack of biscuits and a tin cup to his belt. Then he would take the children by the hand, and the three of them would begin walking. When they would come to a stream, they would eat their biscuits and have a drink out of the tin cup.

At night, the children would help their mother gather firewood and tend the animals. They joined in singing "Come, Come, Ye Saints" around the campfire and slept on blankets under the stars.

They were tired but happy when they finally reached the Salt Lake Valley.

A New Home in the Desert

One of the first things Brigham Young did when they reached the valley was choose a place to build a temple.

The Salt Lake Valley was a hot, dry place when the pioneers arrived.

But they used the canyon streams to water their crops, and they planted trees.

They also built homes, churches, and schools.

The people had to work hard to make a new home in the desert, but they were happy to be in a safe place where they could worship God in peace.

The Miracle of the Seagulls

The second year the pioneers were in the Valley, they planted seeds. They would need the food to feed themselves and all the new members of the Church who were coming to Utah.

But before the crops were ready to harvest, millions of black crickets began eating the young, green plants.

The pioneers tried everything to get rid of the crickets. Nothing worked.

Then the people kneeled in their fields and prayed for help. Thousands of seagulls came and began eating the crickets.

The plants were saved. The pioneers thanked Heavenly Father for the miracle.

Indian Friends

Sometimes the pioneers had trouble with Indians.

Brigham Young taught the Saints that we are all children of Heavenly Father. He told the people to feed the Indians and to help them—not fight them.

Soon the Indians were their friends and not their enemies.

Tithing

When Lorenzo Snow was the prophet, the Church did not have enough money to do its work. On a visit to Southern Utah, President Snow saw how the people were struggling.

It had not rained for a long time, and the crops were dying. Heavenly Father told the prophet to promise the Saints that if they would pay their tithing, they would have rain.

The people trusted the Lord and began paying their tithing. Heavenly Father sent rain, and the crops were saved. Because the Saints paid their tithing, the Church now had enough money to do its work.

Temples

Members of The Church of Jesus Christ of Latter-day Saints know that temples are important. There are many temples in many lands all around the world.

Men and women go to the temple to be married to each other forever. Families go to the temple to be sealed, so they can live together forever.

The temple is a beautiful and sacred place. It is the House of the Lord.

The Modern Church

Today The Church of Jesus Christ of Latter-day Saints has members in almost every country in the world.

Church members love the Savior and want to do what is right.

They are happy to have a living prophet.

They try to be kind and helpful and to be good examples to their friends.

All over the world, thousands of missionaries are teaching the restored gospel.

Latter-day Saints want everyone in the world to know and love the Savior. They hope for the Church to continue to grow.

About the Author

Award-winning, bestselling author Deanna Draper Buck and her husband have been married over forty-five years. They currently live in Hooper, Utah, where they enjoy gardening and entertaining their eight children and their twenty-three grandchildren. Deanna also enjoys quilting. Deanna has written eleven LDS children's books, explaining gospel principles, Church history, and scripture stories in a simplified style.

About the Illustrator

Jerry Harston held a degree in graphic design and illustrated more than thirty children's books. He received many honors for his art, and his clients included numerous Fortune 500 corporations. Jerry passed away in December 2009.